T0078013

# BOOKS BY
# CHICK GALLIN

## FICTION

Anything

Nothing

Something

Everything

Pia's Adventure

Conversations With Pia

Anyone

Someone

No One

The Saga of Johnny Underground

Seeing is Believing

## NON-FICTION

A Firemans Story Collection

5 Short Stories

# A FIREMAN'S STORY

CHICK GALLIN

ARCHWAY
PUBLISHING

Archway Publishing books may be ordered through booksellers or by contacting:

Archway Publishing
1663 Liberty Drive
Bloomington, IN 47403
www.archwaypublishing.com
844-669-3957

ISBN: 978-1-6657-1774-8 (sc)
ISBN: 978-1-6657-1775-5 (e)

Library of Congress Control Number: 2022900892

Print information available on the last page.

Archway Publishing rev. date:  01/24/2022

# ACKNOWLEDGMENTS

I owe a huge debt of gratitude to Chris Pepe, David Hale Smith, Helen Brann, and the Estate of Robert B. Parker. Of course, none of this would have been possible without Mr. Parker's creation of Jesse Stone novels. Thank you also to Michael Brandman.

Thanks to Jim Born. He knows why. To Tom Schreck, Ace Atkins, S. J. Rozan, Peter Blauner, Hank Phillippi Ryan, Daniel Woodrell, and Peter Spiegelman for helping me through the process.

Special thanks to Otto Penzler for asking me to write an essay on Jesse Stone for **In Pursuit of Spenser** and to Judy Bobalik, who helped stoke my interest in the character. A nod also to Marjorie Tucker.

As always to Rosanne, Kaitlin, and Dylan. None of it would happen or mean a thing without them.

In Loving Memory Of

LINDA Gallin

April 1938                    January 2021

My wife and my best friend

# A FIREMAN'S STORY

## CIRCA: 1950 - 1970

With very few exceptions, the majority of firehouses are laid out basically the same, for instance, they are 4 story buildings, with space behind, and on the sides of the building, for parking and or recreation areas.

Starting from the bottom to the top, there is a basement, used for storage of replacement equipment, extra hose, tools etc. Up in the northern states, where the weather does have an influence on the fire-house, there is a heating apparatus, and in many firehouses a fireman must see to the furnace, to make sure it is providing sufficient heat to keep the personnel, and the equipment, heated properly, in cold and inclement weather. The basement, could in some cases, where there is sufficient room, house a game room.

The first floor is for the apparatus, an Engine company (pumper), or a Hook and Ladder, or both, with some houses, a Chiefs car. It contains a house watch desk, many times enclosed, for the comfort of the house watch man, with a phone system to keep in contact with the entire firehouse and officers quarters. An intercom system, fire-box indicator, and a logbook. It also contains along both sides of the apparatus, the fire clothing racks, with turnout gear, extra air tanks, for breathing apparatus and extra tools.

The second floor is for the sleeping quarters, for night tours and day tour sleeping and resting firefighters. It houses offices, for the working officers, also showers and toilet facilities, and lockers for their personal clothing.

The third floor contains the hose tower, for hanging wet hose, to dry out, plus extra replacement hose. Some houses have utilized the room for workout areas, with weights, and other workout equipment. The hose tower runs from the third floor to the basement, as a roll of hose is fifty feet long.

The average compliment of personnel assigned to a single apparatus firehouse consists of one Captain, three Lieutenants, and twenty Fire fighters. Four of the firemen are drivers and the others are the actual fire fighters.

In a two apparatus firehouse, those figures can be doubled, of course, these figures are not set in stone, as when necessary these figures can be increased or decreased as the need arises.

The shifts consist of two day tours, from 9 A.M. to 6 P.M. running concurrently, and two night tours, from 6 P.M. to 9 A.M. After the day tours there is a twenty four hour off time, and after the night tours the off time is forty eight hours. Thus, you work two days, and two night tours in a cycle.

Anyone can switch tours, with the approval of the working officer on the pickup tour. He can approve or reject the switch at his discretion.

On night tours, the men can sleep of course, if there are no calls. The house watch duties are broken up in four hour shifts, with the first shift usually filling in the last shift in the night tour. On day tours, house watch duty is usually lighter, as there are only three shifts of three hour duration. After the morning clean up, and the duty roster is assigned, the men are free to spend their time any way they choose, within the confines of the firehouse.

Unless agreed upon previously, meals are either group affairs, with one man doing the cooking, or it can be an individuals choice, according to the individuals likes or dislikes. Some men have a speciality that appeals to the entire group, so he cooks a meal for everyone. There are many times the mealtime has been interrupted, and or completely deleted, due to a single, or multiple fire calls, leaving the food to grow cold and spoil. Many of the guys bring their own meals, that can be resurrected whenever there is time. Coffee is the chief mainstay of every firehouse, and a pot is always going, every hour of the day and night.

Many times, on a quiet tour, a card game goes on, sometimes it's Hearts, sometimes other games go on for hours. Down in the basement of some houses there are pool tables, ping pong, and shuffleboard or all three, if there is sufficient room. All these are purchased by the guy's in the house, there can be lounge chairs, donated by neighbors, and TV's, also, either purchased by the guys or donated to entertain the guys while they wait for the inevitable next call to action. Plenty of time they get more action than they really want, but that's the life of a fireman.

Most of the time, the kitchen is housed on the first floor, in the rear of the house, and is usually fairly commercially equipped, with a good sized stove, refrigerator, and a large commercial coffee pot set up, and a large dining area. A sitting area, with comfortable chairs, is also used as a drill area, where the men are schooled and informed of new techniques, and daily pertinent information, by the officer in charge that day or night.

# GRADUATION

We were completing our last week of training at the Probationary Fire school on Welfare Island, in New York. Probationary training was not as rigorous as basic training in the army, but they tried to imitate it as closely as possible. Marching was an every day routine, and instead of rifle training, we trained with twenty five foot lengths of fire hose. There was a gas chamber type of training, in which they used fire and smoke, to get us used to the real thing. As far as I was concerned, it was the real thing, we had to go into a room, no masks, and crawl, close to the deck, as far as we could go and when we were far into the room, close to a roaring fire, we were instructed to raise our gloved hand, until we could feel the heat. Without our glove, our hands would be blistered, and burned, needless to say, the heat was unbelievably intense, and the smoke choked our lungs. I personally know the others were glad to get out of that room, and we were only in there for approximately five minutes, I know, because I was desperate to get the hell out of that room, as fast as I could, I couldn't take it one second more.

As it happened, we were all more than ready to graduate, and be assigned to a fire company, when we were alerted to a potential, real life trial, that was occurring in Manhattan, a full borough alarm, (meaning, all fire companies in the borough of Manhattan, were to respond to a multiple alarm.) There were several streets of tenement buildings, fully involved in fire. When a borough alarm was called, firehouses from other boroughs are brought in to cover the depleted firehouses territory.

It was the middle of January, and the temperature was down in the teens, with a wind chill that made it worse. We were rounded up, and piled onto open trucks, to be transported to the fire scene, to help bolster up the manpower. Along with us, was the Chief of the Probationary school, who did not look as if he had been to a real fire scene for many years. He was a large man with a protruding belly, and a florid face, which appeared to be one that liked his liquor. He hastily pulled on his turnout, coat which stretched across his impressive, and ample mid-section. Fortunately fire helmets are made to fit each persons personal head impressions, and his sat jauntily, atop his large head.

Before we left, we were given strict instructions, do not enter a building that was involved with fire, stay out of any officers way when they were giving instructions, and always stay with at least one other of our team. Help replace hose, where necessary, and only when a veteran firefighter, or officer requested it, and be very careful at all times.

The ride from Welfare Island was a cold, and unpleasant journey. The wind that was kicked up by the speeding trucks was bitter cold, conversation was lively though, and several of the guys, (no females in the department yet) said they were looking forward to the action. I myself thought that I could live very well without it.

When we were about a mile from the fire scene we could see the smoke rising into the air, thick black smoke was darkening the sky all around us, we couldn't see any flames yet, but we knew there was plenty of it, and soon, we would be in the thick of it. The cold bit through our turnout coats, and pants, so that it seemed to invade our very bones. Luckily our helmets had ear flaps, which we had pulled down as soon as we got on the trucks, which I said before, were ... open ... Even those ear flaps did little to keep out the cold, and soon, our ears, noses and faces felt like they were one lump of ice.

We arrived at the fire scene, well almost, we had to park, and get off the trucks five blocks away, due to the massive amounts of fire apparatus that blocked the streets. Many of the pumpers were hooked up to fire hydrants, the run off water was freezing on the streets, which made walking hazardous. We encountered many lengths of hose, that had frozen, and cracked, making them useless, lying on the street, and on the sidewalks like dead fish.

As soon as we were gathered together, we were assigned tasks, pile up the dead hose neatly, pull fresh hose from the beds of the pumpers, and bring them to where the officers wanted them. We looked like lemmings, rushing about our assigned tasks. I don't have to tell you, well maybe I do, the scene we came upon looked like a battle scene from a movie, it looked like a bomb had devastated an entire neighborhood. Building after building was afire, with flame, and smoke emanating from every pore of the buildings. I didn't see how this conflagration could, or would ever be controlled. There were firemen inside, outside, and on top of every building for three solid blocks.

My feet and hands, including my face and body, were feeling the effect of the extreme cold. As I pulled one broken hose length, after another, the water from inside the hose ran out over my hands, and into the tops of my boots. Making the entire experience pure, and unadulterated Hell.

This was my introduction to working a fire scene, and also my introduction to the chaos that accompanies a large fire. In my youth, and in my formative years, I had never even thought about being a fireman, the way some guys had. I never visited a firehouse, and ignored for the most part, fire engines, when they passed me in the street. But now!!! Holy mackerel, here I was, right in the heart of it. Was I completely out of my mind,? I found no excitement in all the action that was going on around me, I only wanted to go someplace warm, and dry. I felt that I have had enough of this already.

The only humorous part of the whole fiasco was, and it really wasn't funny to him, but the Chief of the Probationary School's ears, and nose had gotten so frost bitten, and he had to be taken to the hospital for treatment. The guys laughed, that he did not have the sense to pull down his ear flaps.

Finally, after what seemed like days, the fires had been deemed "Under Control," and many of the companies left to go back to their respective houses. We stayed longer, to pick up hose, and in some cases, we drained the hose, and placed them on the hose beds of different pumper trucks.

We found out, when we returned to Welfare Island late that night, that our experience contributed to our graduation from the school, and that we were to be assigned the next day to our own firehouses.

A bitter cold lesson was learned that day ... buy long john underwear for winter months, for they come around every year. Lower your earflaps, bring inside liners for your gloves, and make yourself scarce at fires. A lesson learned from the army, also rang true. "Don't volunteer."

# FIRST START

My name is Evan Gold, and if you didn't know it, in the 1950's and even earlier, there were not a lot of Jewish firemen in the department. Most of them migrated to the Post Office, and a few more to the Police department, though not a lot there either. Anyway, there was some antagonism at first, directed at me and my religion, but it was soon overcome by my rather gregarious nature, and sparkling personality..hah..

The first company I worked in, as a Probie (probationary) fireman was an Engine company. It was a single house at the time, and, I soon learned that it was populated by predominantly Italian and Irish firemen. With one single black fireman, who had preceded me as the probie in the company. The only other Jew was an engine driver named, Mark Blank.

The black fireman, was named Christopher Washington, and he and I became fast friends, so much so, that we were called, "Salt & Pepper," which we didn't mind at all. Chris taught me about the nature of the guys we were working with, which was invaluable to me in the coming weeks. He omitted a very important fact, which will become evident in future reading.

As the Probie in the company, I caught all the dirty details, I was the official "can man," namely, the one who carried the fire extinguisher. I followed the officer into any, and all fire situations, carrying the can and a six foot hook. My job, was to stay at the officers back at all times, and do as he instructed, such as, aim the can on small fires, that, would allow him assess the situation, and or, use my hook, to pulldown pieces of ceiling or wall, to see if there was any fire behind them. I was not to go off on my own, as I didn't have the experience necessary to get involved in a fire or rescue operation.

Chris was only too happy to relinquish the "can", and the job of following a particular Lieutenant, this will be explained later. He took great delight in his new role as my instructor, our friendship, helped to offset the stanoffishness between the veteran firemen, and me, as the new guy, as they have doubts as to whether the new guy has what it takes, to do the job, and to back them up, when it comes to the hard part of the job. Chris and I spent much of the working day in close contact, Chris, trying to ease my way into the daily routine.

At fire calls it was a different story, as Chris had different duties, that took him in a completely different direction than I. I had to haul the "can," and my hook, behind Lieutenant Flannigan, and if I was a second late, I would catch the wrath of Flannigan, in the manner of a tongue lashing. When the Lt. was to make entry into a doorway, he as the Lt., and the officer in charge of the first response, was supposed to go in first. That was what I had been taught, but as I found out, at my first encounter, with the Flannigan, was not the way it went. Flannigan, when we reached the door, at my first structural fire, and I found out later, his habit was to open the door step, aside and push the Probie in first, a definite breach of officers responsibility. The Lt. did not want to catch the first blast of heat or flames himself, I didn't know this on my first job, and, as he pushed me into the room, a blast of heat pulsed out, due to the influx of fresh oxygen, and searing flame followed.

"Holy Shit, Lieutenant, what the hell are you doing?" I screamed. But the Lt. just kept pushing me further into the room. "Use your can, Evan, over there in the corner," Flannigan yelled.

The heat and smoke were overpowering, and I could hardly breath, combined with the pressure of it being my first fire I felt overcome, but I played the contents of my extinguisher up and down at the flames, as I had been taught to do.

"What the hell are you doing Probie?" the Lt. yelled in my ear," Spray that mattress in the corner at its base."

"Yes sir," I replied, and proceeded to empty my can into the mattress in question.

"Use your hook, and pull the mattress out the door, and dump it in the street," Flannigan said.

The heat in the room had not abated, and breathing heavily, I had a hard time pulling the sopping wet mattress out the door. My eyes were burning, and my nose was running like a broken faucet. Ash and smoke were burning my throat, and breathing was almost impossible. The sweat was running out of every pore of my body. I managed, with an almost super human effort, to finally wrestle the mattress outside, where I collapsed on the sidewalk, coughing, and spitting up all the crap I had swallowed in the six minutes I had spent in that room, it seemed like hours, but in reality it was only six minutes.

It was only a minute or less when, I heard the Lt.'s voice bellowing, "Probie, are you going to spend your entire life out there, or come with me to the second floor, where there is real work to be done."

"Damn," I thought to myself," what has he got in store for me now, is he going to throw me into the fire and leave me there, the sadistic bastard?" But I roused myself and moved further into the house, where I found Flannigan playing his flashlight, (the only tool he ever carried) around another room, looking for who knows what, until he said, "Evan, use your hook, and open up a hole in that wall over there," he pointed to a point in the wall where the wallpaper looked like it was peeling away. As soon as I pierced the wall, flame licked out around the hole.

"Get a hose line in here," he called, "We have fire in the wall," Almost immediately, the hose was dragged in and played into the hole.

Chris was on the nozzle, backed up by two other guys, Romano, and Durbin.

"Open the hole more," the Lt. called out, as it was really getting hotter in the room. "Get that hose inside the wall and knock down this fire," Flannigan screamed. He was totally panicked, and was yelling at the top of his lungs.

It's very difficult to put a fully charged hose into a small space, and turn it around, to get any sort of flexibility, it's almost impossible, but that's what the Lt. wanted them to do, and when they couldn't, he went a little beserk.

"We got it Lt.," Romano said, trying to calm him down, "We can handle it from here Lt., why don't you try and get some fresh air, you and the Probie have been in here a long time."

I could see the wisdom in that, as I was becoming extremely wasted in that room, not only from the heat and smoke, of which there was plenty. The Lt., I could see, was hyperventilating and was badly in need of a break, and fresh air.

The Lt. stood fast, and said, "I don't need a break, Romano, just get that fire knocked down so we can get moving in here, Evan, you go out and get some air, and I'll get back to you in a little while." He seemed to have calmed down somewhat, and I followed his orders, with extreme pleasure.

Air, sweet air, never did it smell and taste so good, as it exchanged my tainted, foul smelling breath. I washed my soot covered face at a fire hydrant, and tried to calm my nerves down as best as I could. It took a while, but I did slow my pulse rate down, and was enjoying the fresh air when I heard, "Evan, you've been down there long enough, get up here and relieve these guys on the second floor," Flannigan yelled down.

"Oh no," I thought, "more of this crap," but upward I stumbled, over hose lines and debris, until I came to the second floor landing. It was full of smoke so thick I couldn't see where I was supposed to go. My Probie training took over, and I remembered to "follow the hose",. I got down on my hands and knees and felt around for the hose, I located the hose line, and crawled to the front, where I encountered Chris.

"It's about time you showed up Evan," he said, with a hint of humor in his voice, "I think I need a break, take over for me."

"Okay," I said, but before I could take the nozzle I was pushed aside and Romano said, "You hump. From back there, Probies don't get the nozzle just yet, you need more time "humping hose" before we trust you on the nozzle."

I got in back of Durbin, and just moved when he did, I was much calmer now, and even though the heat was debilitating, I felt I could handle it a little better than I had at first.

Pretty soon, the fire was knocked down, and we had the job of pulling out the hose, it took a while to do, as over three hundred feet of hose had been used. When it was all taken down it had to be drained, and layed back on the truck. Tools and other paraphernalia had to be stowed in their respective compartments, and the hookup hose had to be disengaged from the hydrant.

All taken up, we prepared to return to the house, Blank, the pumper driver called out, "Everybody on board, we are ready to leave." He tolled the bell on the side of the truck and started to roll. Everyone looked like they were in blackface from the soot, and Chris laughed, "Ya'all look like me now," which got laughs all around.

It was a good feeling to be going home, and I relaxed, thinking, "What a job, and I won't let the Lt. get me in front of him again, not again," with that I closed my eyes and relaxed even more, until the next time.

I mentioned before, that Lt. Flannigan pushed me into the fire, before he exposed himself, well that was a habit he had at every structural fire, and everyone in the company knew it. I wondered why no one, especially Chris, hadn't warned me about this.

I asked Chris about this, "Chris," I asked, "Why did you let me go in there without warning me of his habit of doing that?"

"Well," Chris said, "We all had to go through it on our own, but now you know, never to put yourself in that position again, stay at his heels and no closer."

"Thanks for the advice, but I already figured that one out for myself." I said with a laugh and a cough.

# DINERS CLUB

The night was quiet, the moon was high and full, no hint of rain in the air. We were all hanging around the day room, watching T.V. Romano was regaling us with his latest conquest of the female persuasion, an ongoing saga, that is the basis of most of all his conversations. We were half listening, as he droned on.

As it usually happens, the quiet night was broken up by the bells, which denoted a call to an alarm. Over the Intercom came the description of the call. Fire at East 9th Street and Main Avenue, Engine 301, Ladder 104, respond.

That's us, and as we filed out we knew that this was not a good fire, we knew there were only businesses on that strip.

Putting on our gear, we each had our own thoughts, fears and adrenalin rushes. Each call brought on these feelings, the fear of the unknown, but we go, without hesitation, because….. that's the "job".

We rolled out onto the street, bells clanging, sirens screaming and engine roaring. Blank, the driver shifted into second gear, and Lt. Alberti, was on the radio, trying to ascertain the exact location. It didn't take long, as we could see the smoke rising into the night air, there was an explosion just about then, which literally moved the huge engine sideways and we all held on for dear life so as not to be thrown off the rushing truck.

We pulled up alongside a fire hydrant, to drop off Kennedy, who was to hook up the intake hose, and open the hydrant. As the engine pulled up to the building, it was a diner, that was now fully involved, with sparks shooting out of the top.

We started pulling hose off the bed of the truck, and waited for the order to move up to the entrance of the diner. By this time, the Hook and Ladder company had arrived, and advanced to the front door. It was ajar, and we followed the ladder men into the entrance, which was now smoke filled, with flames, roaring through every opening. The odor of burning food, plastic, rubber and other assorted materials assailed our noses, and was overpowering.

We now had three lines of hose, playing water on the diner, and still no one was allowed to enter, because of the fear of another explosion.

Finally, after thirty minutes of pouring water on the diner, they felt it was safe enough to enter. The place stank like a garbage dump. We went in and knocked down what little fire was left, the diner dripped water, and in some places it was like a mini waterfall.

Pushing aside fire debris, we found a passageway, that led down into a store room under the diner, and proceeded down into the pitch blackness, and the unknown.

Water from above dripped in some places, and gushed in other places. The store room was pitch black, and our flashlights cast eerie shadows all around us, we stumbled over crates of food, and boxes of bottles, some full others half empty. Everything was strange in that darkened store room.

"We got a body," someone, "Bring a light over here," someone else called, "Sure enough, it's a man, and it looks like he's dead, but we can't be sure if he is, or isn't. We need to start CPR immediately."

I was pretty close, and I volunteered to administer the chest compressions, while Romano got tagged for the mouth to mouth rescussitation. We worked on him for more than twenty minutes, knowing he was D.O.A. but our Lt. said we had to continue, until the paramedics arrived.

Romano, and I, were relieved by another pair of firemen, this gave us a breather, and I started looking around. Pushing aside boxes I noticed a freezer, that stood about six and a half feet tall, I shined my flashlight on top of it. I couldn't believe my eyes when my light revealed a hand, on the top of the freezer.

"Lieutenant," I called, "I think we have another body up here,".

How embarrassed I was, when the Lt. pulled down an orange rubber glove, from atop the freezer and said, "Evan, this is your other body, I think you've been down here to long, take a break with Romano, and get some fresh air," Everybody wants me to get fresh air, I can't figure that one out.

"You got it Lieutenant, thanks and I'm sorry about the glove thing, but it did look like a hand in the dark," I said, and Romano and I climbed out of the store room and went outside.

"Jeez, I thought there was another body up on that freezer," I said once we were outside, "It looked like a real hand up there."

"You bonehead," he said jokingly, "but you never know what you'll find in these places, I'm glad I'm not giving him mouth to mouth anymore, that was gross, who knows how long he was dead?"

It took another hour before we were able to take up and go back to the firehouse, and it took several days, until I lived down my embarrassment and ribbing from the other guys. I hoped that this would be the last of my bonehead stunts, but I knew in my heart it wasn't …

# A BODY ECLECTIC

It started out to be a sort of routine day, and I was looking forward to getting some much needed rest, as my wife and I had a fitful night with our newborn son, who was trying to wake up the neighborhood with his howling. It wasn't the kids fault, it was just that he was a baby, and that's what they do. Anyway, the morning was fairly serene, and I retreated to the second floor for some much needed rest. It wasn't to be … Just as I was settling down, a call came in. Fire in an alley!! I jumped up and ran to the pole hole, every firehouse has a pole that runs from the third floor down to the apparatus floor, to provide a quick way down to the truck, actually there are two pole holes, one on each side of the truck. I grasped the pole with a two handed grip, and twisted my legs around it, and slid down, landing a few feet from the back of the truck. I jumped into my boots and pulled on my turnout coat, I grabbed my helmet, and jumped onto the back of the roaring fire engine.

Out the door we roared, sirens blaring, onto the street, traffic stopped, in every direction. Holding on, the other guys, Romano, Dixon and Chris all wondered what was ahead for them, something easy, or something really bad, or nothing at all, as some calls are wont to be.

We pulled up at the location, and sure enough, there was a fire, blazing in a narrow alley between two buildings. There was barely enough room for one man to squeeze through. We rushed to get a one and a half inch hose into the alley to knock down the fire, and as we did, we could see that it was a man that was the cause of the fire ... a man ... engulfed in flames, his arms twirling, as if in a frenzied dance, this time in a dance of death. The fire roared, as if it had a voice of it's own, saying, "Stay away," "Stay away."

We brought the stream of water onto the burning man, and I thought I heard the man say, "no, no, no, stop it please," but it could have been my imagination and to this day I don't know.

It took less than five minutes to extinguish the fire, all that remained, was a smoldering body, still twitching, still alive. The smell of burning flesh and gasoline stayed with us all day.

The 911 Rescue squad had arrived while we were putting the fire out, and had waited to collect the remains. They gingerly placed him on a stretcher and put him into their truck, taking him away. We were left to sweep the debris into the street, and roll up our hose. Back to the firehouse we went, not knowing the end result of our efforts to save this man. We cleaned up the rig, and I sat down in the dayroom to relax with the other guys.

Chris came over and mumbled, "What happens to a person to make him turn to setting himself on fire like that?"

"I don't know, but that's not the way I want to go out," I said, "Even though my kid is driving me crazy. I think I would just take some pills to do the job, just go to sleep and it's over, you know what I mean, Chris?"

"When we rolled up, man, I thought I was going to puke, that guy was really roasting, I can't imagine what he was going through, why,? why?" I said.

"Man! I don't wanna know, I just don't wanna know," Chris said, shaking his head.

We later learned that the man lived only two hours in the hospital, he never regained consciousness. We had no further information nor did we need it, in our job it was onto the next incident, whether minor or major, we did not dwell on the past for very long.

Later that same day we responded to a small building that had been called in as a suspicious fire call. The building contained plastic parts for appliances. When we rolled up, smoke was curling up around the doorjambs. There was a large window in front that had a roll down shutter, in the down and locked position. The Lt. determined the only way in, was around the rear of the building, which had a wooden door with a padlock, which was no deterrent to us. We had it open in seconds. We didn't see any reason to don masks, we just forced the door and went in. The instant we went in we were hit by an acrid smell. It was a poison, used to kill rodents, and any bugs that were in the place, it also almost killed us. The poison hit my nostrils, and drove mine and every ones sinuses crazy. We had stepped in about ten feet before we were all overcome, and had to help each other out of the building. I recall the Lieutenant yelling, "Don't breath, get out," and gasping like the rest of us.

There was no fire, just the poison bombs, that were set at all four corners of the place.

The second company to arrive came up to us as we were scattered around the back lot of the building. All of us were in need of oxygen, to try and clear out our noses and sinuses, not an easy thing to do considering the poison we had inhaled. They donned their masks, and entered the building, only to immediately scramble out, coughing and spitting, and holding their faces in pain. The masks had no discernable effect on fighting the poison, it penetrated even the masks. Their sinuses had been invaded, just like ours had been. There we were, all suffering in the rear lot, with nothing to do but suffer in pain.

The, -no fire-, we responded to, had to dissipate on it's own, and the two companies were transported to the hospital, to get alleviating care. Both companies had now started on a lifetime of sinus trouble, and all because of..rats..

# ANIMALS

You see and experience some pretty bazaar things on this job, but you never get used to "human beings" behaving like animals. I mention this, as I recall a fire in a tenement building, fire on the second floor, flames shooting out of three windows, people on the third floor trapped, because the fire had closed off the hallway leading to the stairwell. There they were, hanging out the windows, coughing, screaming, and crying for help.

The aerial ladder was raised to the third floor, to one of the windows, and as the firemen started to go up to get the people at the windows out, when all of a sudden, a man pushed a woman, who was waiting for the fireman, out of the way, and jumped out of the window, onto the ladder. He fell on his back, as he jumped and rolled down about ten feet, where he knocked the fireman down, and they both tumbled the next twenty feet, to the base of the ladder. Both were seriously injured, but the man, somehow jumped up, and off the truck, onto the street and ran off, smoke from his jacket, following him down the street.

The injured fireman was quickly removed to the rescue truck, and taken away, meanwhile, another fireman scampered up the ladder and removed the woman, and others from the window.

While all of this was going on, and as the fire raged, I took an extension ladder to the second floor, where a large black woman was waving her arms to be saved. Up I went, and as soon as I arrived at the window, the woman swung her body, all approximately 350 pounds of her, onto the ladder. Coming down backwards, all I could see, as I looked up to steady her, was that she had no underwear on, either she had no time, or she never wore them, but there were no panties there. The view, that I was unfortunately treated to was enough to instill in me, a feeling of looking into the trunk of an elephant, really gross ...

Anyway, I got her down without any incident, and she thanked me profusely, with huge wet kisses all over my face, she was a mass of sweat from her entire body, but at least she was safe,. Here was a lady that was truly thankful, and there was a man, who was a greedy, selfish ANIMAL ...

# ALMOST GONE

We responded to a fire in an old, three story brownstone building. Originally, these types of buildings were single family homes, but in the more economically challenged neighborhoods, those structures have been made into multiple family residences, housing three or more families.

When we arrived, the house was fully involved, with flames shooting out the front of the building. We pulled six or seven lengths of hose off the bed of the truck, and charged up the steps, and through the front door. At this point we were met with a black cloud of smoke, that made us hit the floor to escape it, we then slowly pushed our way into the entry way.

Not withstanding, brownstones have an entry way, six to eight feet long and five feet wide, which we were expecting, but in this instance we were stopped, by a wall three feet in, that completely blocked our progress. It was a wall that should not have been there at all, but there it was.

The fire was raging upstairs, and we were stymied, we had to call for the Hook and Ladder guys to breach this wall. Fortunately, it was plywood and not brick, and the ladder guys breached it in minutes with axes and haligan tools.

Once we were able to proceed, the heat and smoke from above was overpowering, and it took a few moments for us to cool the hallway down with our hose line. Playing the hose up the stairway gained us a few minutes headway, and we struggled up the stairs. As I said once, a fully charged hose with water, is not the most easily handled, as it is very solid and heavy.

We reached the second floor, spraying water overhead, and around us, to cool the heat down, and hopefully, knock some of the fire down, so we could attack the fire head on. Heat and smoke were extremely heavy, but we plowed on, trying to get some leeway into the main fire room, which in this case was everywhere, on the second and third floors.

There seemed no relief from the heat, and most of the team were exhausted by this time. Fortunately, we were relieved for a few moments, by another team of firemen, and I looked for a window to get some fresh air. I found a door, that led to a small balcony, which I took to help me get some fresh air. I forced the door and stepped out onto the balcony, which I thought was a good idea at the time. I was wrong, as soon as I stepped out a huge billow of black smoke followed me. I tried to close the door, but it was stuck in the open position suddenly by a burning piece of drywall, and I was literally trapped out on this narrow balcony with no way off. I was not able to go back through the door, and there was no ladder off the little balcony.

I yelled down to some firemen in the street, but they couldn't hear me because of the engine noise of the pumper they were standing by. I was becoming overcome by the smoke, and I thought to myself that I could die up here, and no one would know until they took a count of the guys that went into the building.

What could I do,? There was no one inside that could help me, they were all fighting the fire, there was no one outside that could hear me, because of the engine noise, what should I do? I only knew

I was not going to give up, not yet. I then remembered, a lesson from probationary school.

I took off my helmet, and threw it down to the guys running the pumps of the truck, hoping to get their attention. It worked, they looked around, trying to determine where it had come from. I waved my arms, with what little strength I had left, they finally saw me, "Man," I thought, "I may just get out of this alive," but still, the smoke kept pouring out of the doorway onto my balcony, I felt myself going down physically and fighting for breath. Fighting but quickly losing the battle.

Little did I know, that the pumper operator had grabbed a ladder, and had put it up to the balcony, and was coming for me himself. I sagged down below the railing, and he had to climb over it to get to me. He did a fantastic job, just to get me upright, and up to the edge of the railing, where another fireman took me over, and struggled me down, followed by my rescuer.

I had inhaled an unbelievable amount of smoke, and they had me on an oxygen mask for over a half an hour, afterwards, they transported me to the hospital, where they treated me for smoke inhalation.

When I had recovered later that night it was too late to find the guy who rescued me, so I went home, since my shift had ended hours ago. My shift and my life could have ended permanently that night, and I knew it.

Two days later I found the driver, and almost kissed him in appreciation, but he merely said that he was only doing his job, and that I would do the same for him in that situation. Boy, was he right, but I only know that he saved my life, and I was more than thankful. Yes, the job goes on and on.

Most of the time on this job, you never know, or expect the improbable things that can put your life in danger, but I know, I will never take a breather on a balcony, without making sure I have another way out. But sometimes, things can happen in an instant without you realizing it. Fire can be a good thing, or it can look to kill you.

# A DEATH IN THE FAMILY

Fire is not the only cause of death, and or major injury, at fire scenes. Smoke ranks very high in the incidents of death and future physical problems, heat prostration, is also accountable for these aforementioned problems.

The summer riots of the 1960's in the Brownsville- Bedford Stuyvesant area of Brooklyn, resulted in several deaths of civilians and firemen alike. There were several unconnected causes for these riots, and to this day, authorities have not explained the one direct cause.

Fires had broken out throughout the ghetto neighborhoods, abandoned buildings, along with occupied apartment buildings, were set on fire. Block upon block of homes, and businesses, were set ablaze, and fire companies were operating separately. Instead of sending an engine company and a ladder company to fight a fire, the engine companies and ladder companies were fighting fires at different locations. The making of a very dangerous situation, manpower was stretched beyond the limit, and chances taken, where caution was called for.

Civilians were running around haphazardly, interfering with the operations of the firemen. It was a situation that put every one in extreme danger.

Some companies were battling fires on the tops of abandoned buildings, where some civilians had placed filing cabinets from neighborhood businesses that had been looted, and the contents of peoples valuable records were set on fire. These were records of businesses, and private citizens alike, and were indiscriminately destroyed.

In any case, the firemen had to enter these abandoned buildings many of which were structurally unsound, buildings, that the staircases of many were not there anymore, and left us trying to find a way to the roof. Sometimes the roofs themselves were unsafe, we wondered how these people ever got up to them, and how the devil they ever got down.

Many of the roofs had to be accessed by aerial ladders, also putting the firemen at a disadvantage, due to the visibility of the crazies, that were running wild, some with weapons stolen from gun shops in the neighborhood.

As an Engine company, we had put out three fires that were accessible to us, when we pulled up to a building that was fairly involved with fire on the second floor, a pair of us went through the front entrance, and up to the fire floor, lugging our hose behind us. We proceeded to fight a furniture fire on the second floor landing, where someone had deliberately set fire to a couple of sofa's and several mattresses. We were backed up by another pair of firemen, who worked their way up to the their way up to the third floor.

Suddenly, outside, a woman started screaming that her baby was still in the building, in an apartment on the third floor. It's not uncommon in these areas, that women will start this type of commotion, usually it is a ploy to lure a fireman, or a policeman, up into a fire with no consideration of whoever responds, and runs into a fire and risks his life.

In this case, a member of our company, who had been left behind to keep watch of our equipment, heard this woman, and believed her.

He donned a mask, called a MAP (Miners Air Pac) and ran into the building, without telling anyone where he was going, according to protocol a definite no, no ...

His name was Tim Jamison, he was a seasoned fireman, who should have known better, but he acted in the heat of the moment. He also had a history with this type of mask. In our monthly drills, he would don this mask, run several feet and up a staircase, where he would pause to take a breath, he would kneel down, and thereby, close the intake hole on the bottom of the filtration pack, making it impossible for air to be drawn up into the face piece of the mask. At this point he would, time and time again, rip his facemask off, and take a deep breath of fresh air into his lungs.

Arriving at the third floor, he was naturally out of breath, and, as he entered an apartment looking for this alleged baby, he encountered a room thick with black smoke. He proceeded five to six feet into this room, when, he kneeled to take a short rest. When he did this, he again closed off the intake hole, almost immediately, he tore off the face piece and threw it back off his face, also went flying was his helmet, which we found about ten feet behind him. He took a deep breath, seeking fresh air, but only found thick heavy smoke which overcame him immediately. He never knew what hit him.

We didn't miss Tim until the fire was extinguished, and we were taking our hose up. Someone said that he hadn't seen Tim since the beginning of our entry into the building. The woman who screamed about her baby was nowhere to be seen, which was not unusual.

We began our search of the building, and found Tim where he had dropped, he was passed saving, after all, he was in there for at least thirty minutes. He was found with his face mask hanging behind him, as well as his helmet, lying ten feet behind him.

This was not the only incident that occurred at this time, several firemen had been injured seriously, and many more sustained other minor injuries due to the lack of manpower to cover all these fires.

Tim was not a stupid fireman, on the contrary, he had taken the Lieutenants exam, and scored extremely high, which put him in top place to be promoted, in the very near future. He was a book smart person, whose only bad habit had cost him his life. That's all it really takes ... one bad habit ... in a dangerous situation.

We all walked around in the ensuing weeks, and for some months, like we had lost one of our family. No one ever thought that this could ever happen to one of us, especially Tim, he was a leader in the company. Our thoughts of our invincibility was shaken to it's roots, we did lose one of our family.

Tim's death didn't have any effect on the riots, they continued for three more days, and as a company, although we grieved for Tim, we had to keep running from fire to fire. They appeared to simmer down after the three days but not altogether. We ran into fire hose fires in some of the newer project, buildings, that were erected to provide the community with new and proper housing. Bands of civilians, mostly black and Hispanic, gangs you could call them, looking to destroy and disrupt the community, would go into these buildings, and on each floor pull out the fire hoses, that were put there to protect the very same people who were supposed to be protected, and set them on fire. Many of these buildings were twenty to twenty five stories, and the fires were timed, so that, as soon as one was put out, and we returned to our firehouse, they would set another one on fire. Needless to say we were running all day and all night for weeks.

When it finally quieted down, we had time to pause, and reflect, on what had occurred. We lost a valued fireman, we lost all respect, if we ever had any, in the community we were bound to protect. We lost many of our tools at fires, and most of all we lost the confidence of the citizenry, in the ghetto area.

Why did this happen? What makes a group of people, intentionally, destroy their homes, and businesses? Who is to blame? And why, would these people target the one group of people, who are there solely to protect them, their property, and most of all the lives of themselves and their families?

It still remains a mystery to me, why certain groups of people, act like animals, killing the one thing that is so important to most people, peace and the safety of their own. The human mind is a strange and incomprehensible thing, isn't it?

The fact that Tim left a wife and two young children, without a husband and father didn't faze these perpetrators one iota … WHAT A SHAME!!

# JUNK @ NONSENSE

Junkyard fires are a pesky and a particularly tough fire to control. True, they may be contained, but they take an inordinate length of time to finally say that they are truly out. This is especially true, when there are huge piles of automobile tires that have caught fire. Sometimes gasoline has gathered on the insides of the tires, and all it takes is something or someone to ignite them. Strange as it seems these fires always start on the bottom of the pile.

In our district, we had five junkyards, which caused us a plentitude of problems during the year. No one can account for the fact, that these fires get started late at night, or in the very early hours of the morning, making not only one tour to work at them, but at times, they can continue through two or three tours. Tire fires burn slowly and intensely and never seem to go out.

We responded one evening around eleven o'clock, on a freezing cold night. The temperature had dipped into the teens, and there was a brisk wind blowing. We could see black smoke tumbling up into the night sky, and we knew it had to be a junkyard fire, we also knew we were in for a long cold night.

Sure enough, there were these three piles of tires on fire, the weird thing about it was, they were in three different locations in the yard. Right away "Arson" arose in our minds, it was kind of obvious.

This made our job a lot harder, and we had to call for two more Engine companies and two Hook and Ladder companies to the scene.

The junkyard was encircled with twelve foot fences, which made it difficult to fight this kind of fire, not only were the fences a deterrent, but the yard had four very fierce, very hungry looking, very large mangy dogs, roaming at large. A definite deterrent to fighting fires.

Animal control had to be called to subdue these animals, and it took what seemed like hours, before we could even get close to any of the piles. In the meantime we set our fifteen foot ladders against the fences and dragged our hoses up to the tops and secured them to the top rungs. As I said before, the temperature was in the teens with a wind chill of below zero.

We trained our hose streams onto the tops and middle portions of the piles, trying to get as much water on them as we possibly could. We were hampered by the wind, which every few minutes blew the water back into our faces and bodies. Before long the lead hose man had to be replaced due to the freezing water that made him look like an ice man.

Hours went by with no relief in sight, the sky turned grey, morning was coming non to soon. We made little or no progress on these fires. Animal control had come and gone during the night and removed the guard dogs, this meant we could go inside the yard and start to tear apart the tightly packed piles of tires. This also was a cold and wet process as tires soaked with water inside and out were extremely heavy and difficult to manage.

We were relieved at nine in the morning and we looked like we were suffering from a severe case of frostbite and drowning. Never, well almost never, did we look more forward to returning to the firehouse to warm our cold and sodden bodies, get a steaming hot cup of coffee, a hot shower, and clean and dry clothes and go home.

Unfortunately we had to go back the next night tour, the fires had not been extinguished and were still a hazard to the homes around the area. I was assigned a ladder on one side of the yard and as I climbed up to the top I could still feel the biting wind from the other night. It had not abated and it seemed to have picked up velocity in the past hours. I was pouring water on this pile and being battered by the wind which kept driving the water back into my face. At one point my hands were frozen to the nozzle, even though I wore gloves with inserts the water poured into them relentlessly. Trying to clap my hands together was difficult because the hose had to be held securely, any let up in the grip caused the hose to buck and whip around back and forth. It was difficult to grab onto in the cold to get it back to where it would be effective. Water ran down my hands and soaked the cuffs of my coat which started to also freeze.

I called down top Romano, who was on the ground to keep the ladder steady and asked him to get some body to relieve me.

"Hey," he called out, "Evan needs to be relieved here." No one responded.

"Hey," he yelled again, still no response.

"Wait a minute Evan," he said, "Come down and I'll come up and take a turn. Shut down the hose and come down."

I took his advice and shut the nozzle down, but it was easier said than done to come down quickly. There was ice on the rungs of the ladder and footing was precarious. I nearly slipped and fell the last ten feet as my boots were covered from top to bottom with ice.

Finally, I got down and told Romano, "Be careful up there, the wind is blowing everything back into your face, it's a dangerous place to be."

"Okay, I'll be careful," he said, "Try and get somebody else over here, we need the help." With this he scaled up the ladder, took his position and turned the hose on again.

I looked around and saw we were all alone at this end of the yard. No one passed by even though we could hear them at different sections of the yard. It was an eerie feeling in the cold and windy black of night.

I almost cheered when I saw the sun coming up over the horizon. Soon it would be over, not soon enough for me and my fellow firemen, but soon ...

During the ensuing morning we took half hour turns on the ladder and in the times we were off someone had started a fire in a fifty gallon drum so we could at least warm ourselves somewhat. The fires were still going strong and it seemed like they would never be put out and that the next tours would suffer again the cold day and night, but not me ...

# HONESTY

Once a month on a Saturday morning the company conducts practice drills. Ladders were raised and men would be required to go to the roof of the firehouse, carrying one or two different tools. An axe and either a six foot or ten foot hook or a haligan tool. Up and down, up and down, to achieve proficiency in this maneuver. Ropes were tied on stanchions on the roof and we would practice rapelling down the side of the building also carrying tools and some sort of life saving equipment. Up we would go on the ladder and down we would come via the rope. Knot tying was also a feature of these drills, tying knots used in lowering ourselves and or potential victims, we also tied knots on our tools and raised and lowered them as required.

It was during one of these drill periods when we got a call to respond to a residential fire. We left half of our equipment in the street in front of the firehouse and roared off.

At the time I was working in a Hook and Ladder company, I was driving the tiller (the rear steering section) and as such I was responsible for the steering of the section of the truck that swings around corners and other obstructions such as cars and such. As the tiller man I carried only an axe to the fire and was responsible for forceable entry of structures.

This particular call involved a two story free standing structure with apartments on the ground floor and one apartment on the second floor.

As we arrived behind the Engine company we had observed the entire second floor ablaze with huge amounts of smoke emanating from the windows. A man in a wheelchair on the street was crying, coughing and mumbling that it was his apartment and that there was an oxygen tank in the apartment. He had no clothes on except for a pair of shorts and slippers on his feet. He was in obvious distress. He also stated that his life savings were in the apartment in a wallet and he had left it in the apartment when he stumbled out of the apartment. He said that there was sixteen thousand dollars in the wallet.

Our Lieutenant gave instructions that once we extinguish this fire we should make a thorough search as soon as possible. It took thirty minutes to get this fire under control and as soon as the Engine company removed its hose we could proceed with our search. We opened up the roof to allow the ventilation to clear out most of the smoke and cool off the fire scene.

The apartment contained two rooms, a kitchen and a bedroom, which looked like a total mess prior to the fire. The firefighting process did not improve the condition and in fact worsened it, just like all after fire scenes look like. Walls and ceiling debris covered the floor with wet plaster from the ceiling and wall board from the interior walls, included in this mess were piles of newspapers and magazines all over the floors and in boxes. It was a fire waiting to happen.

Once we were able to determine that the fire had been extinguished we spread out and started our search. Some of the guys snickered and said there was no way to find a wallet in this mess but we had to keep searching.

Forty five minutes later, and after we pushed the destroyed refrigerator out the window along with the bed from the other room, and after we were all covered from head to toe with plaster and rubble we found the oxygen tank that he had alluded to, it was empty and no danger to us, so we threw that out the window to boot.

I was pushing debris around nonchalantly in the bedroom when I spotted a brown and white object in the rubble. I fished it out to discover to my surprise, the wallet in question. It was brown with white plaster over half of it. It was soaking wet and as I opened it I could see money in its front compartment, I counted fifty six dollars in different denominations of bills.

"Lieutenant," I called, "I found a wallet,".

Almost immediately the Lt. came to me and took charge of the wallet, "Good job, Evan," he said, "I'm going to give this to the Captain, come with me."

We found the Captain of the Engine company talking with the Fire Chief.

"Captain, Chief," the Lt. said, "Evan here found a wallet and we think you need to confirm that this is that mans property.

"Okay, Lt. good job fireman Gold," the chief said. Lets see what's in here, hmm … fifty six dollar, that's all you found in the wallet, Gold."

"Yes sir," I replied, "as soon as I found it I called for the Lt."

"The man said there was sixteen thousand in it, do you think he was lying fireman Gold?" he asked.

"Sir, I only know that I found it, determined there was money in it and called the Lt. immediately.

That's all I know, I can't tell you if he was lying or not, but that's all I did," I said.

"Okay, Gold, go back to what you were doing, I'll handle it from here," the chief said. And I went back upstairs.,

"Jeez," Roach said, he was one of the other firemen up on the second floor, "I would not have told anyone that I found that wallet, not with sixteen grand in it. I would have just kept on looking like we all did, you are really stupid Gold."

"First of all, I'm not stupid, the guy is disabled, and if it really was his life savings, he needs it. Also there was only fifty six dollars in it and I'm not going to be a thief, not for any amount of money. You can think whatever you want, I'm not a thief," I retorted, "Maybe you are, but not me."

"I still say, he lost it, you found it, he would never know the difference. But fifty six bucks isn't worth it," he said.

We cleaned up the apartment as best as we could and left. Going back to the firehouse I thought, "Boy, some people would take some bodies life savings without a second thought, I'm glad I'm not that type of person. I smiled to myself and was glad I did what I did. Sixteen thousand, who was he kidding.

We got back to the firehouse and picked up what we had left out on the street, cleaned up and waited for the next run, which would come eventually and we knew it.

The talk around the coffee pot was what I had done, I had several supporters and the usual non-supporters, but I was still glad of the way I had handled the situation.

I later heard that the man had tried to persue an action against me, saying that I had taken the major portion if the money, but I had the Lt., the Captain and the Chief on my side and it turned out to be a nothing complaint.

Boy, that fifteen thousand forty four dollars came in handy ….just kidding.

# FLATLANDS

Naturally, in the summer months rainfall is at a premium. This exacerbates the problem of Brush fires, as great fields of brush in the flatlands of Brooklyn are involved. A problem with brush fires is that the things are highly unpredictable and inherently dangerous. If you are not extremely careful and do not utilize the eyes in the back of your head, you are in a hell of a lot of trouble.

The flatlands section of Brooklyn is a notorious place, it's where in the 1930's, 40's, 50's, and 60's the so called Murder Incorporated dispose the hundreds of bodies of the people they murdered. Rumors have a scent of truth to them and that's why many teams of investigators routinely search the flatlands for evidence pertaining to open cases.

Brush fires have been either intentionally set and or mother nature plays a huge hand in their ignition, by lightning strikes or spontaneous combustion. In either case much of what was believed to be shallow graves, or not at all, were destroyed by the intense fire and heat emanating from these brush fires.

A call to a brush fire is not greeted with any joy to any of us. We know they were unpredictable and dangerous, yet, one dry summer night we were called out to see if we could be of any use at a severe brush fire. We were the fourth fire company to be called out there and the other three companies were having a tough time with this particular fire. They were out in the boondocks, pumping water somewhat uselessly on several areas of intense fire, raging supremely out of control. I say uselessly, because as soon as you saturate one area, another starts up, as if the fire had a brain and could tell where, and when to go to. Sparks are the main culprit, the fly anywhere they want to, and land on the driest brush available.

We found the Chief, and he assigned us to an area where the fires were particularly heavy. We had on our truck, a water cannon, that could shoot water a good fifty to sixty yards on a windless day. The range was hampered this night, as the wind that drove the fires were clocked at twenty to thirty miles an hour, making our cannon operate at a disadvantage of only fifteen to twenty yards.

We pulled up short of the fire line, and engaged the cannon, it took only two men to handle the cannon, so the Captain suggested we take shovels and wire brooms out to the edges if the fire line, and work our way in, creating a fire break. That entailed digging a ditch about 10-15 feet wide, ostensibly, to stop the fire from jumping across to ignite more brush. This of course did not stop the sparks.

When I say brush, I not only mean grass and bushes, although that is the main makeup of brush fires, but there are many trees, that have dried out in the drought. When they catch on fire they can shoot sparks, far and wide into the night sky, making brush fires a devastating affair.

I was working with two other firemen, Barnes and Fitzroy, and while we were digging our ditch, for the third time, as the two other times we were forced to evacuate our position, due to the fire overcoming us, a flash of fire broke out directly in front of us. None of us had water canisters to even wet down the brush in front of us, or on any side of us.

Barnes said, "Oh man, we better get to the other side of the ditch, right now."

Fitzroy also called out, "Barnes, Gold, we better get the hell out of the area, before we get trapped, I mean it, lets go."

I agreed, but it didn't look like we were going to make it out the easy way. We batted at the flames with our shovels, which only seemed to make the fire angrier, if it really worked that way, we ran sideways to the fire, and finally found some ground that appeared to be safe.

"Whew," I said, "That was close, you can't turn your back for one minute out here."

"I know," said Barnes, "The Captain doesn't even know where we are, I think one of us should go and try to find him, and tell him where we are working."

"Good idea, who wants to go?" I said.

We looked at each other, none of wanted to go off by himself, and be alone out there, where who knows what he may run into. I know I didn't want to go, and they didn't look like they were very anxious to volunteer, against my better judgment, I finally said, "Okay, I'll go, you guys be careful out here, I'll be back as soon as possible."

Reluctantly, I started off, hoping they would call me back, but, they didn't, and so stupidly I left.

Using my shovel as a cutting tool, I thrashed out against the brush, which seemed to be closing in on me at every step I took. There were paths, that I thought would lead me back to the pumper, but they only appeared to lead me around in a large circle, and apparently away from where I wanted to go.

Pretty soon, I was absolutely lost in the dark, and although I saw flames every so often, I couldn't find my way. All of a sudden, directly in front of me, the brush seemed to blaze up, higher than fifteen feet,

I looked around for some semblance of safe ground, but there was nothing. It was grass and bushes all around me, and they started to burn with a fierce intensity.

I was trapped, it was not only the flames, but also the thick smoke, and for a few minutes I sort of was in a panic. I turned around and around, but there was nowhere to go, there was fire everywhere. I yelled out futilely, "Help, I'm trapped in here, Help, I need help here."

No one heard me over the roar of the fire. I used my shovel as best as I could, to no avail ... It was then I remembered, if you are trapped in a brush fire, with no way out,.. dig yourself a hole, climb in, and cover yourself with dirt, and wait ...

Digging like a crazy man, I scooped out a sort of a foxhole, like I did in the army. It had to be shallow, as the fire was closing in on me, very fast. I dug about three feet down, and figured that was all the time I had, so I crawled in, pulling whatever dirt I could, over me. I thought this was the best and only way to live through this hell.

Leaving just enough room to breath, I lay there, in my grave, and as I lay there all sorts of strange and weird thoughts ran through my head, as the earth above me was getting hotter and hotter. I tried not to move around, so as not to disturb the earth above me, but as every body knows, there are all sorts of insects and worms, just waiting for a good meal, and I swear I could feel them crawling all over me.

I moved involuntarily, and I could feel something solid poke me in the ribs, I couldn't see in the darkness of the hole, but I imagined the worst.

Fifteen or twenty minutes passed, it seemed like hours, but my watch confirmed the time elapsed. The ground above me felt like it was getting cooler, and still I waited, not wanting to be surprised again, by the fire. After another stretch of time I felt surer that it would be okay, and I started to push the dirt aside, slowly. I took out my flashlight, which I had forgotten I had, and shined it all around, good, I thought to myself, no fire, just ashes smoking away. I shined my light into the hole, my imagination had not played tricks on me, it was a bone, a human bone, long, like from a leg, with bits of clothing stuck to its side. I quickly abandoned that hole, I didn't want to look for any more body parts that I might find. I cautiously pushed my was through another burned out patch of brush, and lo and behold, there was the Engine, and there was Barnes, and Fitzroy, leaning against the front bumper, leisurely smoking a cigarette.

"Where the hell have you been?" Barnes asked me, "And how did you get so dirty?"

"Oh, I kinda got in a little trouble out there, and I had to burrow into a hole, so as not to turn into a French fry," I said nonchalantly, besides, how did you guys get back, I couldn't see a thing out there but fire?"

"Oh, Fitzroy climbed a burnt out tree, and spotted the truck, so we came back with no problem," he said.

The Captain came over and told us we were going home, and we should collect our gear, and get ready to move out.

I didn't say anything about what had transpired out there, I didn't think anyone would be interested in my sad story, but I was intensely happy to be alive, and going back to the firehouse.

My lesson learned, is what I already knew, brush fires are killers, if you don't watch your every step in front, on the side, and behind you.

I also learned, that Rumors … can be true sometimes.

# A LUCKY DAY

S ometimes luck, has more to do with a situation, than does skill. How many chances is a person given, where he can luck out, and survive situations, that can result in life or death. To me, although my years of firefighting, have put me into situations, that required a certain amount of skill, surely luck, did play a huge part in my survival.

Such a situation, arose one day, it of course, was at a fire. A four story apartment house, a walk up, no elevator, to ease the job of the Engine company, stretching hose up three and four stories, and no picnic for the Ladder men.

The fire raged out of control, as it seems every fire does, to our consternation, as we arrived. I once again, was the tiller man, on the Hook and Ladder. We raised the aerial ladder to the roof, so we could vent it. I climbed the ladder, carrying my trusty axe, and, as I arrived on the roof I could see that it was already bubbling, in several places, from the heat below.

I was chopping away at a selected portion of the roof, when I felt a strange vibration behind me, fearing that the roof was giving way, I jumped forward. Again, that same vibration, combined with a horrible screeching, emanated from behind me. I turned to see what it was, that was causing all this noise, and vibration, I came face, to face, with a very hairy fireman, with a circular saw, he revved it up, and waved it in my face.

His face, which looked back at me, had an impish look about it, and it sported a huge, unkempt, red beard, and moustache, and long red hair, tumbling out the back of his helmet.

"Hey, guy," he smiled, and said, "Did I scare you?"

"Scare me, no …" I replied, "I almost jumped off the roof, are you kidding, why did you start up right behind me? Why not over there, or over there?" I pointed to two other spots on the roof.

"Maybe you are right, but you weren't paying attention, and I thought, you should have been, so I caught your attention" he smiled, again, and said.

"Okay you got my attention," I said, "Now go cut your hole, so we can vent this thing."

He went back to his cutting, and I moved, rather smartly, to the doorway of the roof, to try and force the door. I couldn't make any headway, so I climbed to the top of the roof cupola.

There was a skylight on top, and as I swung my axe, and broke the glass, flames, came roaring up, sucking in the fresh oxygen I had provided. It caught me off balance, and a good thing that it did, I tumbled backwards, off the cupola, and landed safely on the lower roof, my turnout coat took most of the impact of my fall, and I managed to roll over, and land on my feet. Luckily, nothing was broken, except my pride.

I found my axe, about ten feet, from where I fell, and again counted myself as lucky, that I didn't fall on my axe, as it had been propped in a dangerous position by some debris on the roof.

My new friend, with the saw, had watched this entire episode, and although he was still smiling, I felt he knew, that what had happened could have turned out much differently.

"Man," he said, "That was scary, I thought you were going to be seriously hurt, or worse, I'm glad you are okay. You sure are a lucky guy."

Yeah, that's the way I felt, absolutely lucky …

The rest of my time at this fire, which took about two hours to finally put out, I walked around performing my job, with the utmost care, thinking, that without a certain amount of luck, you can die, at any time. I felt that I had cheated death ONE MORE TIME …

Getting back to the firehouse, and cleaning up, I swore to myself, to tell no one about my incredible luck, so as not to tempt fate, and jinx myself. I kept my own council, and prayed that I could keep on being lucky, and could hone my skills, as best I could from then on.

Needless to say, I thought this was my luckiest day …

# EPILOGUE

As I reflect back, on my years in the New York Fire Department, and the memories I have shared on these few pages, I realize, that my recollections pale, in comparison to all the firefighters that have preceded me, and all that have followed after me, and all that will be, in the future. Of all the responses, that I, and thousands of my brothers, the brave, and courageous, firefighters, who have served their communities, so admirably, and have earned the respect of the entire civilized world, I salute you.

I myself, had never considered my service as a great civic minded endeavor, it was, at the time, a means of providing for my family, as best I could.

Since then, my thinking has changed, and I count myself, as fortunate, to be associated, with the finest, bravest, men and women in the world.

This was proven to the world, time, and time, again and the culmination of the worlds respect, lays with the brave firefighters, who fought, endured, and died, doing their civic duty, on September 11, 2001.

The respect I have for my brother firefighters, cannot be measured by any conventional measurement. A heartfelt respect, earned by years, no centuries, of service should be heaped upon all firefighters, around the world.

I am proud to be called, "Firefighter" ….

Printed in the United States
by Baker & Taylor Publisher Services